Pakistani AMERICANS

SPIRIT
of America®

Pakistani AMERICANS

By Angela T. Koenig

Content Adviser: Karen Leonard, Ph.D., Department of Asian American Studies,
University of California, Irvine

The Child's World®
Chanhassen, Minnesota

8

Pakistani AMERICANS

Published in the United States of America by The Child's World®
PO Box 326 • Chanhassen, MN 55317-0326 • 800-599-READ • www.childsworld.com

Acknowledgments

The Child's World®: Mary Berendes, Publishing Director

For Editorial Directions, Inc.: E. Russell Primm, Editorial Director; Sarah E. De Capua and Pam Rosenberg, Line Editors; Elizabeth K. Martin, Assistant Editor; Olivia Nellums, Editorial Assistant; Susan Hindman, Copy Editor; Joanne Mattern, Proofreader; Matthew Messbarger, Ann Grau Duvall, and Deborah Grahame, Fact Checkers; Tim Griffin/IndexServ, Indexer; Cian Loughlin O'Day, Photo Researcher; Linda S. Koutris, Photo Selector

Photos

Cover/frontispiece: Courtesy of the Khan family

Cover photographs ©: LWA-JDC/Corbis

Interior photographs ©: Angela Koenig: 17; Baldev/Corbis Sygma: 25; Corbis: 6 (David Samuel Robbins), 7 (Roger Wood), 8 (Stapleton Collection), 11 (Setboun), 12 (Museum of History & Industry), 18 (Paul Barton), 20 (AFP), 22 (Ed Kashi), 27 (John Scheiber); Courtesy of the Khan family: 14, 15, 16, 24; Courtesy of Saghir Tahir: 26-top; Getty Images: 13 (Per-Anders Pettersson), 21 (Tim Boyle); Getty Images/Spencer Platt: 19, 28; Michael Marsland/Yale University: 26-bottom; Reuters NewMedia Inc./Corbis: 10, 23.

Library of Congress Cataloging-in-Publication Data

Koenig, Angela T.
  Pakistani Americans / by Angela T. Koenig.
     p. cm. — (Our cultural heritage)
  "Spirit of America."
  Includes bibliographical references (p.) and index.
  Contents: Pakistan yesterday and today—Pakistan's road to independence—Coming to America—Pakistani impact on America.
   ISBN 1-59296-017-0 (lib. bdg. : alk. paper)
   1. Pakistani Americans—Juvenile literature. [1. Pakistani Americans.] I. Title. II. Series.
   E184.P28K64 2004
   973'.04914122—dc21
                          2003004289

13   24   28

Contents

Dec. 2003 Davidson 19.00 Town

Chapter ONE

The Birth of Pakistan

PAKISTAN IS A COUNTRY IN SOUTH ASIA. IT IS located on the Asian **subcontinent** and is rich in natural resources and history. The country is nearly twice the size of California and about four times the size of Great Britain. It is sometimes called The Land of the Indus. The mighty Indus River, about 1,800 miles (2,897 kilometers) long, runs the entire length of the nation. The Pakistani people also call this river The Lion.

The Indus River runs the entire length of Pakistan.

Throughout history, the rich lands along the Ganges and Indus Rivers have supported agriculture. The area also attracted others who fought to take over the fertile lands for themselves. The first people known to live in this area were called the Indus Valley civilization. These people occupied the land from about 2500 B.C. to 1700 B.C. They built

The ruins at Harappa are the remains of a large city that was part of the Indus Valley civilization.

7

The Mughal Emperor Jahangir and several of his attendants

homes and streets, along with water and sewage systems. These settlements were very advanced for their time. But little is known about this civilization, and what happened to it remains a mystery.

Next came the Hindu kingdoms. Hinduism is a religion and philosophy still widely practiced in India. Then, in **medieval** times, kingdoms ruled by Muslim immigrants from Central Asia, Turkey, and Iran controlled the area. In the 1500s, the Mughal Empire took over. In the 1600s, the British East India Trading Company came to the region. However, it was not content to just trade with the people. The British eventually decided they wanted total control of what was then the country of India. In 1858, the British government put a leader, called a viceroy, in charge of the day-to-day government of the country. In 1877, Queen Victoria was named the Empress of India.

The people of India were not happy being ruled by foreigners. Many people banded together to demand independence from Great Britain. But Indian **nationalist** leaders had different ideas about the future of the country. Hindu leaders Mohandas Gandhi and Jawaharlal Nehru and Muslim leader Muhammad Ali Jinnah disagreed about whether Hindus and Muslims could get along in an independent India. Members of the two different religions had a long history of disagreement.

Finally, the British gave India its independence. The land was partitioned, or divided, along religious lines. The partition granted Muslims their own country, called Pakistan, in 1947. About five million Muslims left India for Pakistan. Nearly four million Hindus and Sikhs **migrated** to India. The division of land did not end the fighting, however. Today, Muslims, Hindus,

Interesting Fact

▷ Islam is one of the
fastest-growing
religions in the
United States.

and Sikhs in India and Pakistan continue to
fight each other. They all live under the
constant threat of nuclear war.

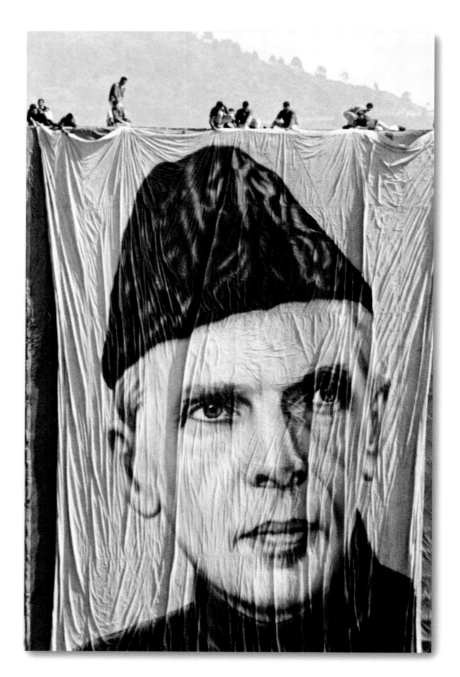

*Pakistani soldiers hanging
a banner of Ali Jinnah, the
founder and first head of
state of Pakistan*

PAKISTANIS ARE PROUD OF THEIR RELIGION—ISLAM. THE WORD *ISLAM* MEANS "submission to God." Followers of Islam are called Muslims. The founder of Islam, Muhammad, was born in the Saudi Arabian city of Mecca in A.D. 570.

Muslims live by five rules, called pillars:

• Creed, which is the belief in one God, Allah, and his prophet, Muhammad.

• Prayer, which is required five times a day.

• Fasting, which means to abstain from, or go without, food and drink from sunrise to sunset during the holy month of Ramadan.

• Charity, which requires all Muslims to donate part of their income to the poor.

• Pilgrimage, which means every Muslim who can afford it must travel to Mecca—the most sacred city in Arabia—at least once in a lifetime.

Friday is the Muslim holy day. Followers gather at mosques to pray. There are more than 1,200 mosques in the United States. Many have been built because of the rise in immigration from Muslim countries such as Pakistan, Afghanistan, Iran, Iraq, and Egypt.

Coming to America

IN THE EARLY 1900S, ASIANS FROM THE INDIAN subcontinent began coming to America in very small numbers. These new immigrants

Some Asian immigrants found work in sawmills, such as this one in Hoquiam, Washington.

often came into the United States from British Columbia, Canada. They made their way south to the western states of California, Washington, and Oregon. There, they worked on the railroads, in lumber mills, and on farms.

Between 1901 and 1910, as many as 5,600 immigrants arrived from India. They faced **discrimination** in many forms. For instance, in California, a law was passed that said Asians could not own land. Then, American immigration laws changed, and it

In the 1960s, most people in Pakistan were living in poverty.

A group of military officers from the Pakistani army trained in the United States in the 1950s. Some of these men immigrated to the United States and joined the U.S. Army.

became nearly impossible for people from South Asia to come to the United States. For the next 60 years, few immigrants from India or Pakistan arrived in America.

Meanwhile, the new country of Pakistan had gotten off to a difficult start. By the 1960s, there were still not enough jobs for everyone. Most people were living in poverty. Schooling was poor. Many children left school at young ages to work on family farms. As a result, half the people in Pakistan could not read or write. Pakistan's economy was struggling. The country had trouble establishing a **democratic** government, and military leaders often took charge. The threat of war with India was constant. These circumstances continue today.

Wanting a better life and more opportunities for themselves and their children, some Pakistanis decided to leave their country permanently. Some moved to the countries of Canada and Australia. Most arrived in the United States, especially after 1965, when U.S. immigration laws became less strict. The new immigrants were mostly well-educated professionals.

A group of Pakistani Americans in Texas the 1970s

15

The greatest number of Pakistanis, about 140,000 arrived in America between 1990 and 2000. In 1990, there were only about 91,889 Pakistani Americans. Today, there are approximately 500,000 Americans who either have come from Pakistan or whose parents or **ancestors** came from Pakistan. Almost as soon as Pakistanis arrived in the United States, they began making a mark on American society.

Many Pakistani Americans came to the United States to seek a better education for their children.

IN MANY WAYS, HUMZA DESHMUKH IS A TYPICAL SEVENTH-GRADER. HE LIKES to eat chocolate chip cookies and plays on a soccer team, called Orange Crush. His 10-year-old sister, Hadiya, also enjoys soccer and is learning Spanish. What makes Humza and Hadiya unique, however, is that they are second-generation Pakistani Americans. They were both born in America. But their parents immigrated to the United States in 1976 from Pakistan, making them first-generation Pakistani Americans.

Reminders of Pakistan are everywhere in the Deshmukh home. Live jasmine trees grow in containers. Jasmine is the national flower of Pakistan. It gives off a fragrant smell. Ornate, embroidered, silk pillows are tossed about for comfort. Wool carpets lay across the floor, and **calligraphy** art hangs on the wall. Embroidery, rug making, and calligraphy are Pakistani handicrafts. An eye-catching miniature bus sits on a bookshelf. In their homeland, buses are wildly decorated to attract passengers.

This family is just one example of the many Pakistani American families who have chosen to call the United States home. It is a small, but growing, ethnic minority. Like nearly all children of immigrants, Humza and Hadiya try to keep what is special about their Pakistani culture as they embrace their life in the United States.

Chapter THREE

Pakistani Americans Today

Many Pakistani Americans are highly educated. A good number of Pakistani American have become doctors.

PAKISTANI-AMERICAN IMMIGRANTS ARE AMONG the most educated people in the United States. Many of them become doctors and business professionals. The Association of Pakistani Physicians of North America (APPNA) estimates there are 10,000 Pakistani-American doctors in the United States. Most every hospital has at least one Pakistani American on its staff. Dr. Ayub Khan Ommaya is a professor at George Washington University in Washington, D.C. He is the inventor of several medical tools. The Ommaya Reservoir, named for him, is used to deliver medicine to the brain.

Pakistani Americans also find careers in the service industries. Nearly 50 percent of America's motel industry and around one-third of the hotel industry are owned by Pakistani and Indian Americans. In large cities, driving taxicabs is also a popular way to earn a living.

This small ethnic minority lives in close-knit communities throughout the United States. The majority of Pakistani Americans live in California, Texas, New York, and Illinois. In New York, an annual Pakistani American parade takes place in August. The parade celebrates Pakistan's independence in 1947.

South Asian traditions have begun popping up in American culture. Celebrities,

A group of Pakistani Americans in Brooklyn, New York, marching in support of the United States after the September 11, 2001, terrorist attacks. New York City has a large Pakistani-American population.

Mehndi being applied to the hands of a group of women

like Madonna, for example, have been photographed wearing mehndi. Mehndi are designs made on the body that look like lacy tattoos. They are made using a dye called **henna.** The designs, which are temporary, are applied for special occasions, especially weddings. A mehndi ceremony, in which the bride's hands and feet are painted with beautiful designs, is traditional at Pakistani weddings.

Prior to the terrorist attacks on September 11, 2001, Pakistani Americans were quietly blending into U.S. communities. After the attacks, small pockets of anti-Muslim attitudes surfaced in America. Nearly 75 percent of Pakistani Americans are Muslims, but the rest are Hindu, Christian, and other religions. Muslim **mosques** were vandalized. Some people were mugged, even killed. Although some people believe that all Muslims hate Americans and will use violence against them, most Pakistani-American Muslims wish for peace everywhere.

The owner of a Pakistani-American video store in Chicago showing his support for the United States after the September 11, 2001, terrorist attacks

AFTER THE SEPTEMBER 11, 2001, TERRORIST ATTACKS, MANY PAKISTANIS WERE worried about their relatives in the United States. Because the attacks are believed to have been carried out by Muslim **fundamentalists,** some people took out their anger on Muslims in the United States. Some Pakistanis feared that their loved ones would be harmed or that they would not be able to practice their faith.

To calm these fears, a group of prominent Pakistani Americans planned a trip to the country where they were born. They wanted to talk to people about their life as Muslims in the United States. These Pakistani Americans,

like members of many other ethnic groups in the United States, are proud to be considered Americans. But they also have strong ties to their native country and Pakistani culture.

The trip took place in November 2001. The group spoke with many people in Pakistan about their experiences in the United States. One member of the group said that when he came to America, there were two mosques in his area. Now there are more than 100. He believes this is a symbol of the freedom of religion found in America. Like many Pakistani Americans, the travelers hope that one day the same level of tolerance and respect for other religions will be common in Pakistan.

Chapter FOUR

Pakistani Impact on American Life

A Pakistani-American family enjoying a traditional meal of kabobs, eggplant, and basmati rice

THOUGH PAKISTANIS ARE RELATIVE NEWCOMERS to the United States when compared to other ethnic groups, their influence on American culture is growing. Pakistani restaurants can be found in many large cities. Delicious foods such as samosas—meat or vegetable filling wrapped in dough and fried—are served. Another popular Pakistani dish is boiled curry chicken. Curry is a mixture of spices popular in

many kinds of South Asian cooking. Pakistani food is often served with the traditional flatbread known as naan.

Qawwali is religious poetry set to music. It is a traditional Muslim religious art form popular in Pakistan. Qawwali has influenced music in the United States and around the world. It has even found its way into musical scores for American movies. Nusrat Fateh Ali Khan, a master singer of qawwali, performed on the soundtrack for the movie *Dead Man Walking.*

A Pakistani-American business owner, Saghir Tahir, made political history in 2000.

Nasrat Fateh Ali Khan (far left, front) performing traditional qawwali music

Interesting Fact

▸ In 2002, President George W. Bush hosted the first ever Ramadan celebration at The White House. Ramadan is the Muslim holy month. President Bush invited Muslims from many countries to participate.

He won a seat in the New Hampshire State Legislature. This is the first time that a Pakistani American has been elected to a high public office.

Saghir Tahir was re-elected to the New Hampshire state legislature in 2002 despite much anti-Muslim sentiment in the United States.

Sara Suleri Goodyear was born in what is now Pakistan when it was still under British control. She is a professor of English at Yale University and a novelist.

The city of Chicago has been home to Pakistani American Tariq Malhance since 1972. In 2002, he was appointed city **comptroller.** Like many other successful Pakistani Americans, he is well educated, holding advanced degrees in the fields of finance and economics.

Sara Suleri Goodyear is an author and professor of English at Yale University.

Fazlur Rahman Khan came to the United States from the part of Pakistan that is now the country

26

of Bangladesh. He attended the University of Illinois in the 1960s and became a prominent engineer. He was the chief engineer for two Chicago landmarks—the Sears Tower and John Hancock building.

Fazlur Rahman Khan was the chief engineer on the team that built the Sears Tower in Chicago, Illinois.

27

The country of Pakistan has existed only since 1947. This makes Pakistani Americans one of the newest groups of immigrants to the United States. Like most Americans, they truly appreciate the freedom and opportunities that they enjoy in America. As they blend into U.S. society, we can all learn to appreciate and enjoy the beauty and richness of the culture they bring with them.

Pakistani Americans, like all U.S. citizens, appreciate the freedoms and opportunities available in the United States.

2500–1700 B.C. The Indus Valley civilization inhabits the Indian subcontinent.

1500s A.D. Muslim invaders inhabit the Indian subcontinent, and the era of the Mughal Empire begins.

1600s The British East India Company begins trading in India and eventually takes control of the region.

1877 Queen Victoria becomes the Empress of India.

1947 India gains its independence. The British divide the lands along religious lines, creating the Muslim nation of Pakistan.

1970–1980 The first big wave of Pakistani immigrants arrive in America. Many are professionals, such as doctors and engineers.

1971 Civil wars break out in Pakistan, and East Pakistan becomes the independent country of Bangladesh.

1990s The second big wave of immigrants arrive in America. About 140,000 Pakistani immigrants became U.S. citizens.

2000 Saghir Tahir, a Pakistani American, is elected to the New Hampshire State Legislature.

2001 Following the September 11 attacks on the United States, Pakistan's president declares the country's support in the U.S.-led war on terrorism.

2002 A Pakistani American, Tariq Malhance, is appointed city comptroller of Chicago, Illinois.

ancestors (AN-sess-turs)
Ancestors are family members who lived long ago. Today, there are approximately 500,000 Americans who have come from Pakistan, or whose parents or ancestors came from Pakistan.

calligraphy (kuh-LIG-ruh-fee)
Calligraphy is the art of beautiful script handwriting. Calligraphy is a traditional Pakistani art.

comptroller (kom-TRO-ler)
A comptroller is a person who works for a government or corporation and is in charge of making sure the group's financial accounts are accurate. The comptroller of the city of Chicago, Illinois, is a Pakistani American.

democratic (dem-uh-KRAT-ik)
In a democratic organization or society, all the members have a say in how things are run. The country of Pakistan has had difficulty establishing a democratic system of government.

discrimination (dis-KRIM-in-ay-shun)
Discrimination is the practice of treating certain groups of people unfairly or unequally because of an unreasonable dislike or distrust of them. Immigrants from South Asia faced a lot of discrimination when they first came to the United States.

fundamentalists (fuhn-duh-MEN-tuhl-ists)
Fundamentalists are people who insist on a very strict interpretation of a group's basic laws or principles. It is believed that Muslim fundamentalists were responsible for the September 11, 2001, terrorist attacks on the United States.

henna (HEN-nah)
Henna is a reddish-brown dye that is made from the crushed leaves of the henna plant. Henna is used in the art of mehndi.

medieval (mihd-EE-vuhl)
Medieval means having to do with the period of time—about A.D. 500 to 1500—known as the Middle Ages. Muslim kingdoms controlled the Indian subcontinent during medieval times.

migrated (MYE-grate-ed)
To migrate is to move from one place or region to another. In 1947, many Hindus and Sikhs migrated to India from Pakistan.

mosques (MOSKS)
Mosques are buildings that are used by Muslims for worship. Muslims gather at mosques to pray.

nationalist (NASH-uh-nuh-list)
A person who is proud of his country or who fights for its independence is called a nationalist. Indian nationalist leaders had different ideas about the future of the nation.

subcontinent (suhb-KON-tuh-nuhnt)
A subcontinent is an area of land that is part of a continent but geographically or politically distinct. Pakistan is located on the Asian subcontinent.

Web Sites

Visit our homepage for lots of links about Pakistani Americans:
http://www.childsworld.com/links.html

Note to Parents, Teachers, and Librarians:
We routinely verify our Web links to make sure they're safe,
active sites—so encourage your readers to check them out!

Books

Caldwell, John C. *Pakistan.* Broomall, Penn.: Chelsea House Publishers, 2000.

English, Karen, and Jonathan Weiner (illustator). *Nadia's Hands.* Honesdale, Penn.: Boyd's Mills Press, 1999.

Khan, Rukhsana. *Ruler of the Courtyard.* New York: Viking Children's Books, 2003.

Places to Visit or Contact

Embassy of the Islamic Republic of Pakistan

2315 Massachusetts Avenue, N.W.
Washington, DC 20008
202/939-6200

Pakistani-American Association of North America (PAANA)

200 East Rand Road
Mt. Prospect, IL 60056
www.pakwatan.com

Index

About the Author

ANGELA T. KOENIG EARNED A B.A. IN COMMUNICATION FROM the University of Kentucky and completed the secondary English education program at the University of Louisville. She is currently a regular contributor at *The Cincinnati Enquirer* and is a freelance correspondent to *People* magazine. She lives in Ohio with her husband and their two young sons.